WITHDRAWN

DRAW 50 PRINCESSES

BOOKS IN THIS SERIES

DRAW 50 PRINCESSES

THE STEP-BY-STEP WAY TO DRAW SNOW WHITE, SLEEPING BEAUTY, CINDERELLA, AND MANY MORE

**Lee J. Ames
and
Holly Handler Moylan**

BROADWAY BOOKS

NEW YORK

PUBLISHED BY BROADWAY BOOKS

Published in the United States by Broadway Books, an imprint of The Doubleday Broadway Publishing Group, a division of Random House, Inc., New York. www.broadwaybooks.com

Library of Congress Cataloging-in-Publication Data
Ames, Lee J.
    Draw 50 princesses : the step-by-step way to draw Snow White, Sleeping Beauty, Cinderella, and many more / Lee J. Ames, Holly Handler Moylan. — 1st ed.
        p. cm. — (Draw 50)
    1. Princesses in art.   2. Drawing—Technique.   I. Moylan, Holly.   II. Title.   III. Title: Draw fifty princesses.   III. Series.

    NC825.P74A44 2008
    743.4'4—dc22

                                                            2008001535

PRINTED IN THE UNITED STATES OF AMERICA

ISBN 978-0-7679-2797-0 (HC)
ISBN 978-0-7679-2798-7 (TP)

10 9 8 7 6 5 4 3 2 1

First Edition

**Our
Don QuixArmstrong who...**   **...reached the
unreachable
stars!**

For Roger, with love
1917–2007

To the Reader

Before you begin drawing, here are some tips on how to use and enjoy this book:

When you start working, use clean white bond paper or drawing paper and a pencil with moderately soft lead (HB or No.2). Have a kneaded eraser on hand (available at art-supply stores). Choose any one of the subjects in the book that you want to draw and then very lightly and very carefully sketch out the first step. As you do so, study the finished step of your chosen drawing to sense how your first step will fit in. Make sure the size of the first step is not so small that the final drawing will be tiny, or so large that you won't be able to fit the finished drawing on the paper. Then, also very lightly and very carefully, sketch out the second step. As you go along, step by step, study not only the lines but also the size of the spaces between lines. Remember, the first steps must be constructed with the greatest care. A wrongly placed stroke could throw the whole drawing off.

As you work, it is a good idea to have a mirror available. Holding your sketch up to the mirror from time to time can show you distortions you might not see otherwise.

As you are adding to the steps, you may discover that they are becoming too dark. Here's where the kneaded eraser becomes particularly useful. You can lighten the darker penciling by strongly pressing the clay-like eraser onto the dark areas.

When you've put it all together and gotten to the last step, finish the drawing firmly with dark, accurate strokes. There is your finished drawing. However, if you want to further finish the drawing with India ink, applied with a pen or fine brush, you can clean out all of the penciling with a kneaded eraser after the ink completely dries.

Remember, if your first attempts do not turn out too well, it's important to keep trying. Practice and patience do indeed help. I would like you to know that on occasion when I have used the steps for a drawing from one of my own books, it has taken me as long as an hour or two to bring it to a finish.

—Lee J. Ames

DRAW **50** PRINCESSES

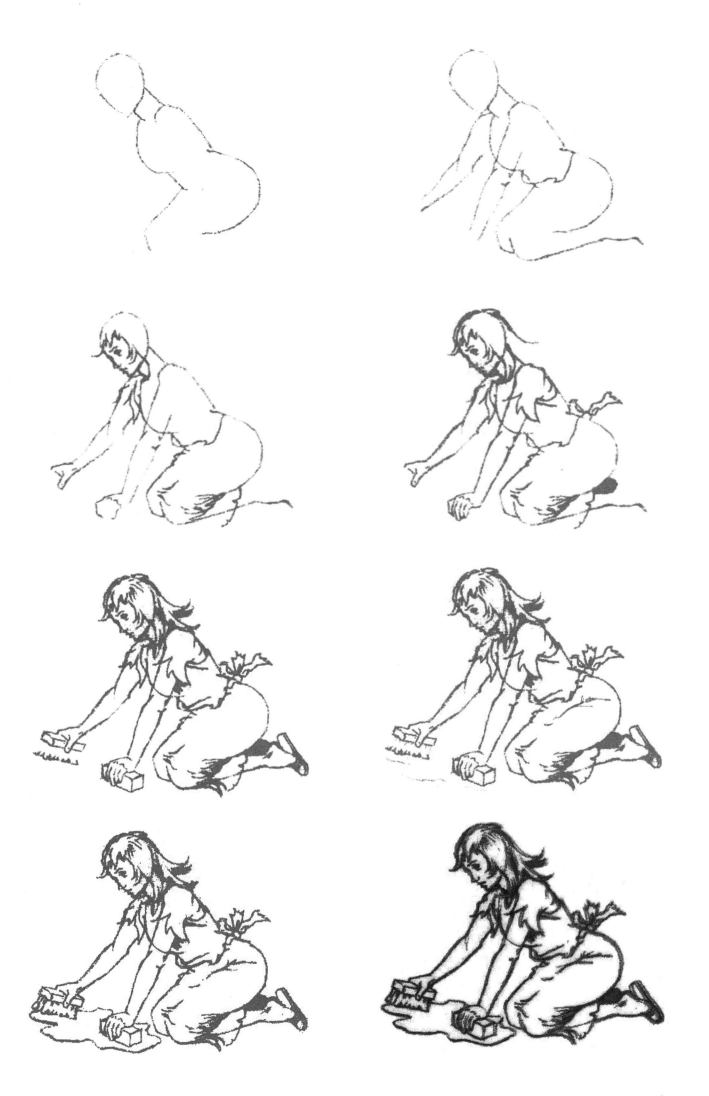

Cinder Ella

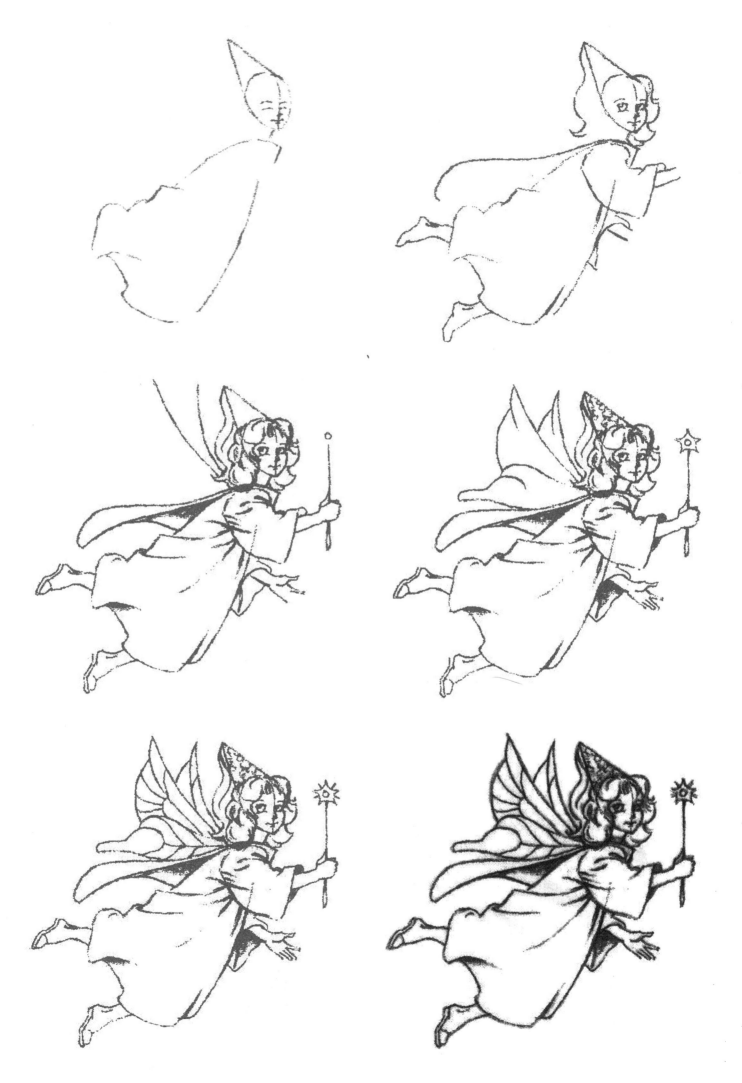

Fairy Godmother

Cinderella

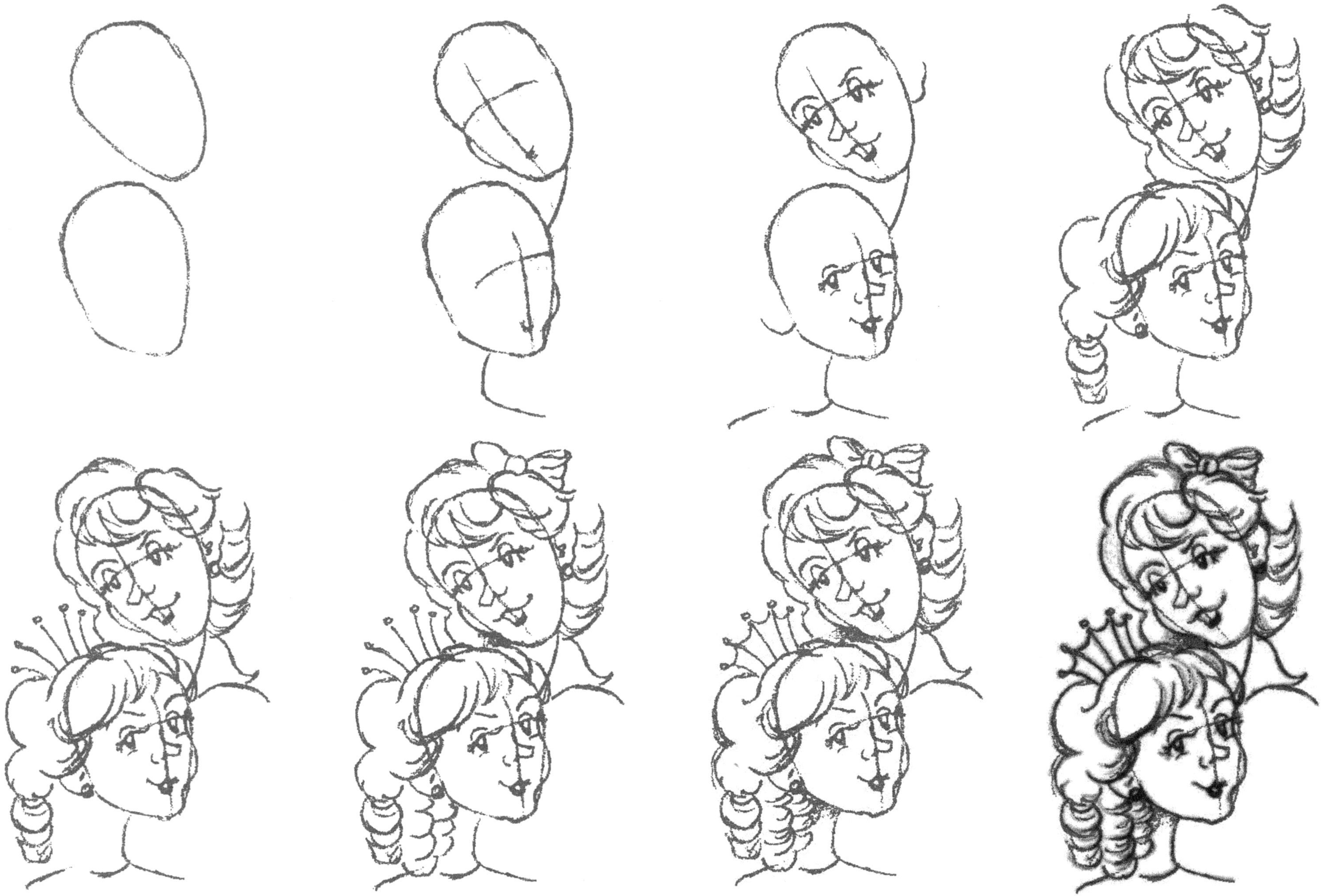

Nasty Stepsisters

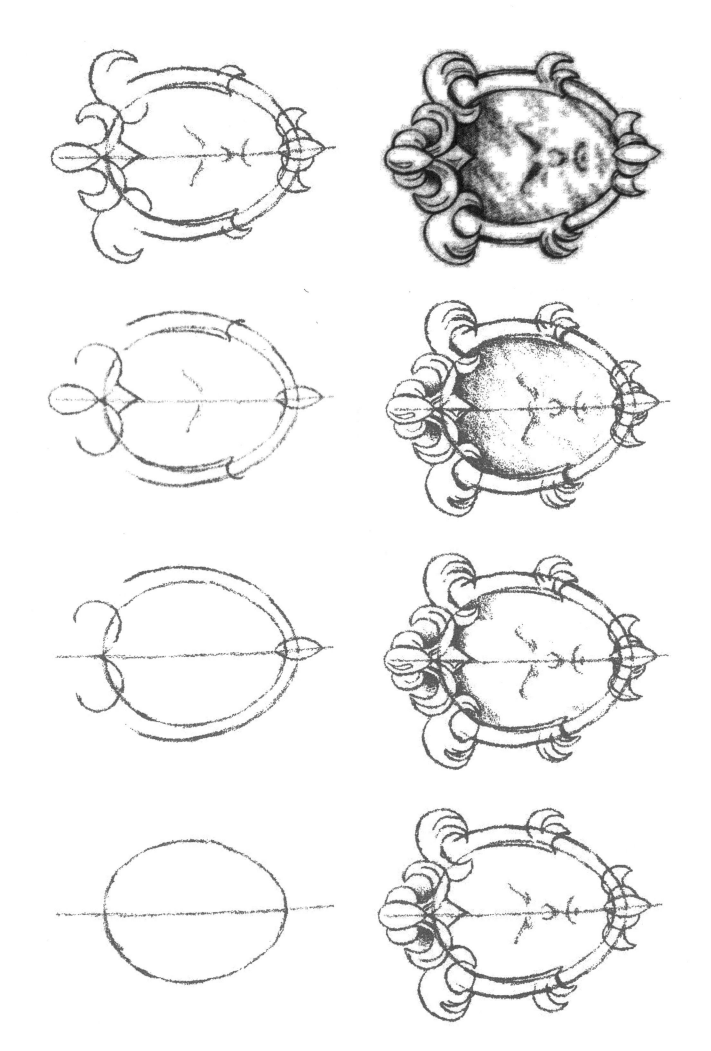

Evil Stepmother

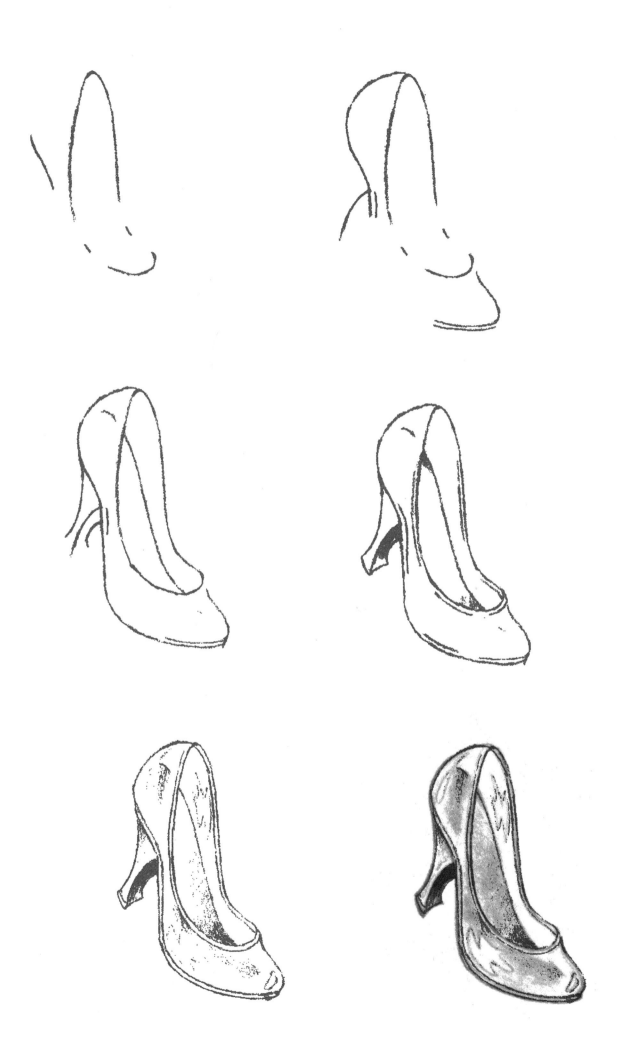

Glass Slipper

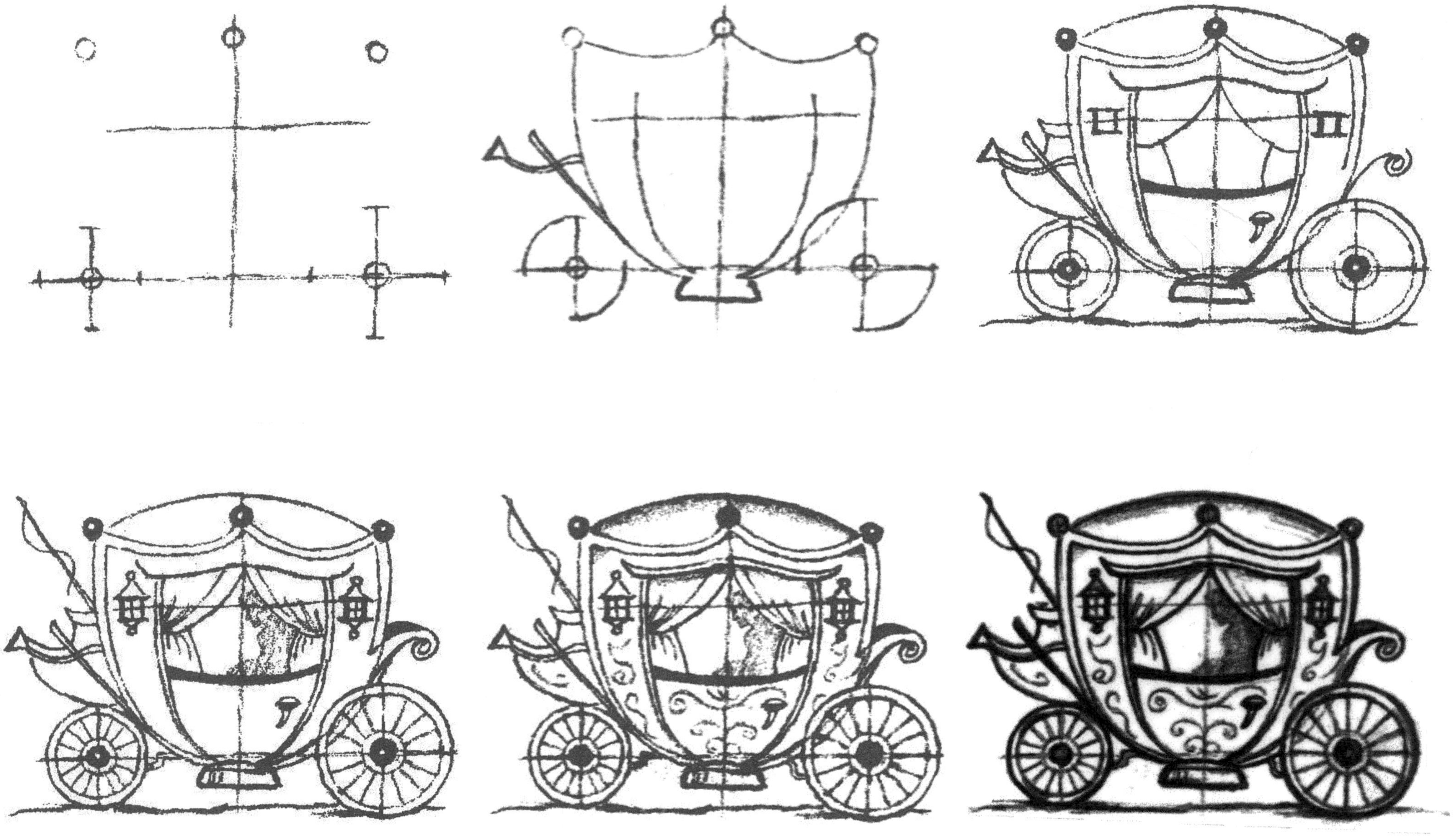

Royal Coach

"Sire, a lost slipper!"

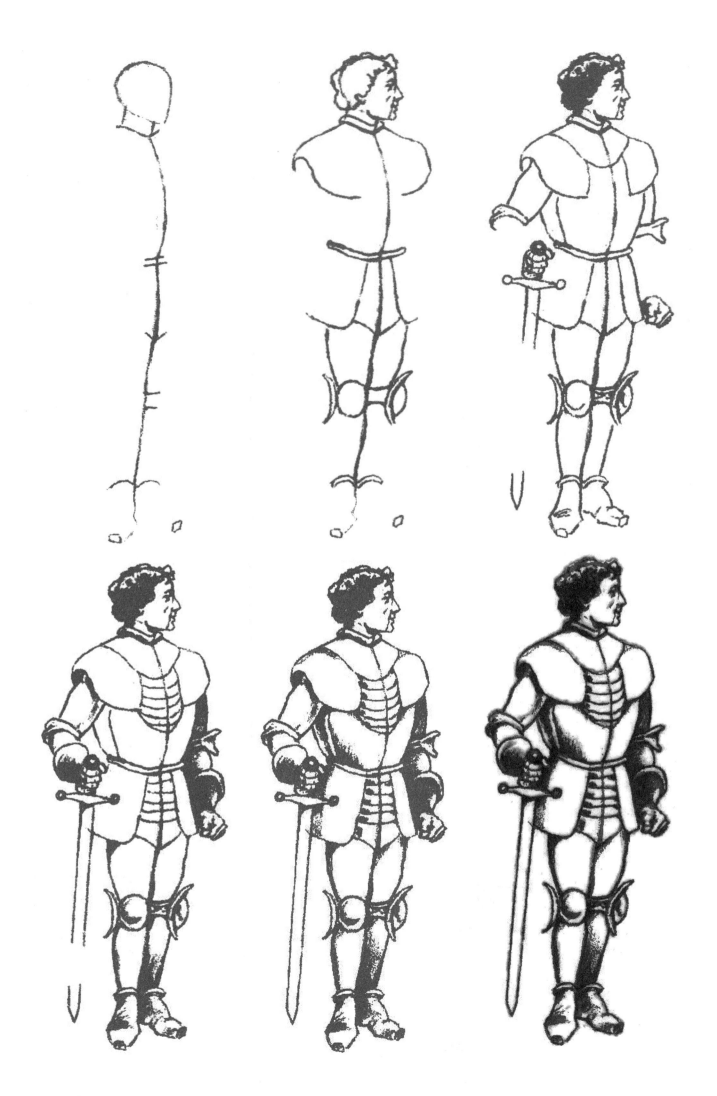

Sir Lancelot

Guinevere

"Lancelittle"

Dragon

Merlin

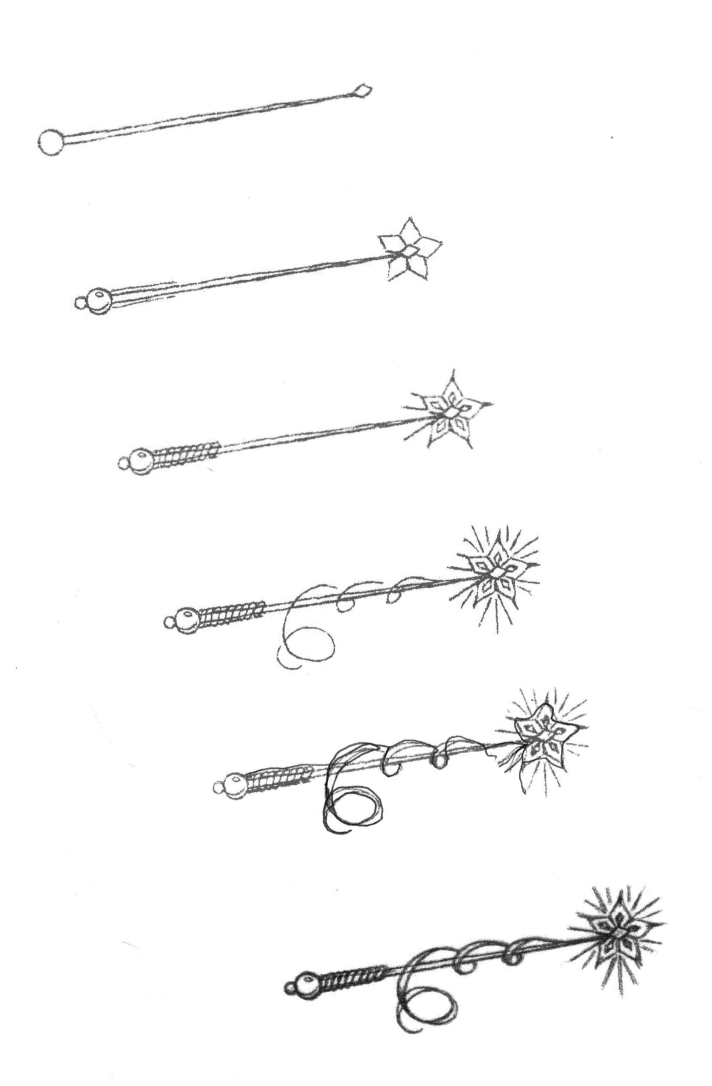

Magic Wand

King Arthur

Goblet

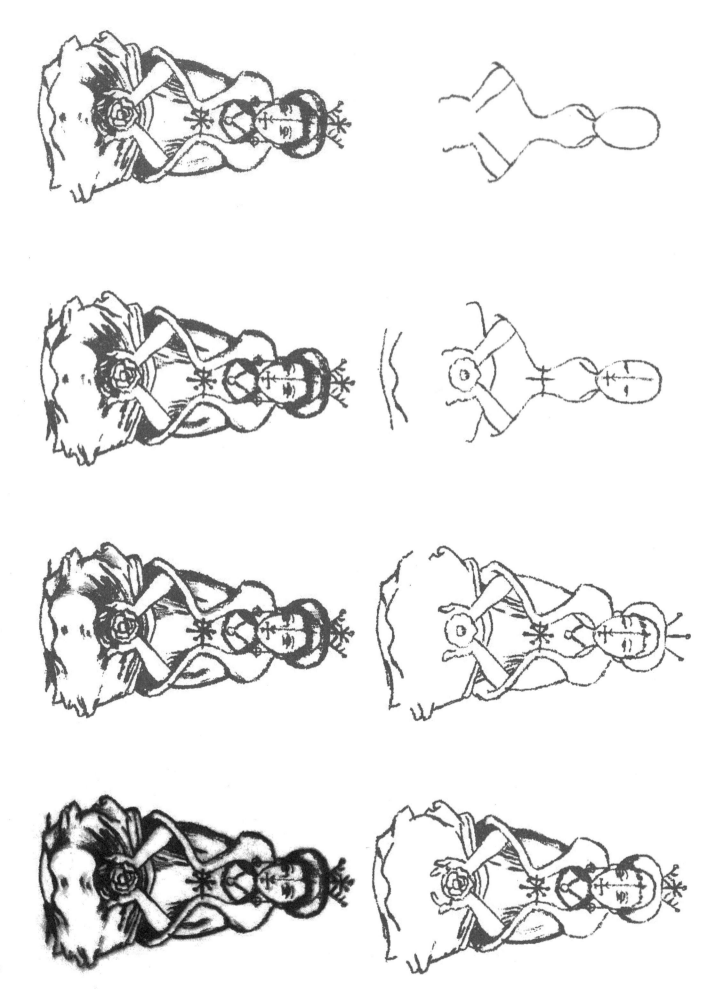

Native American Princess

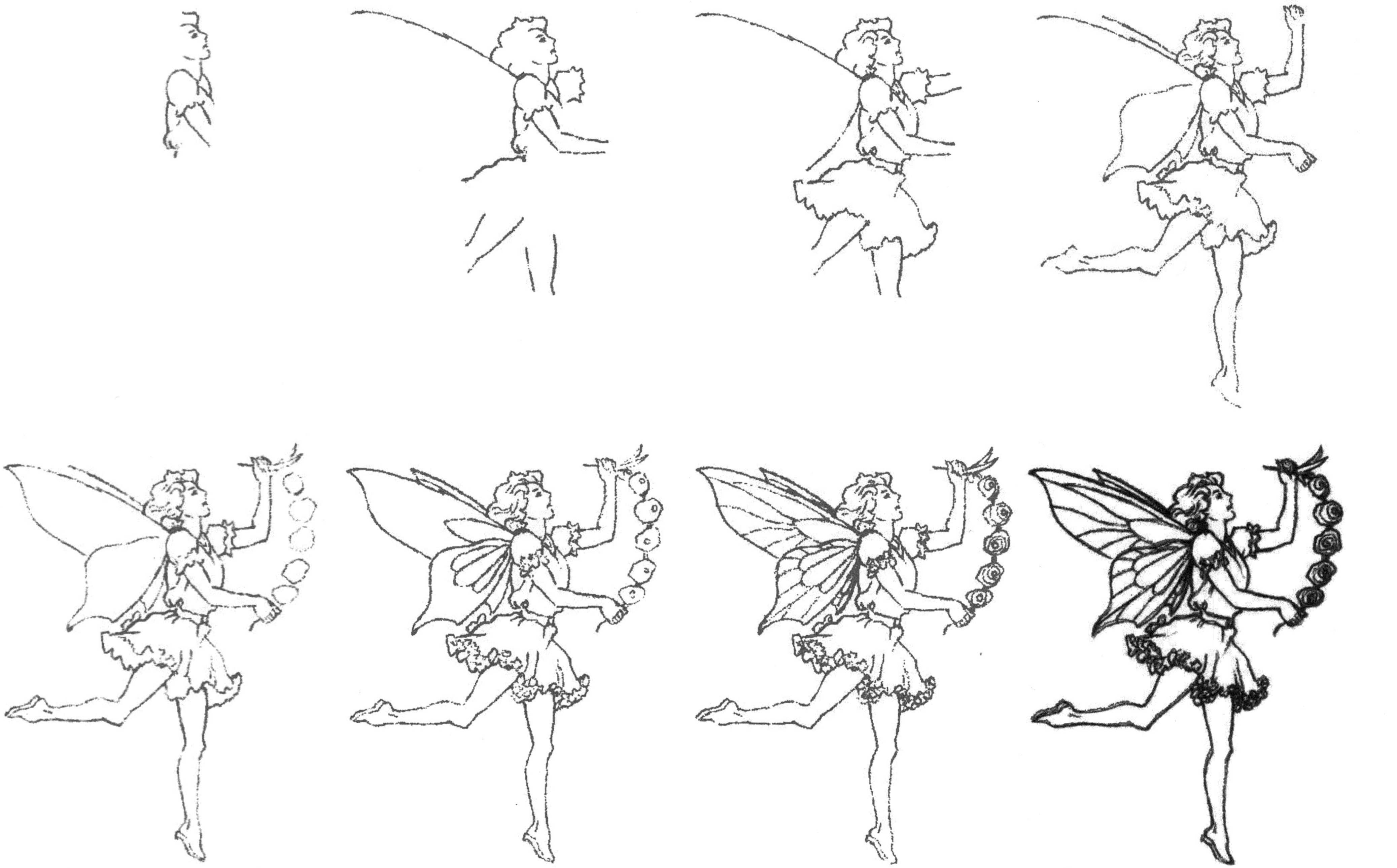

Fairy Princess

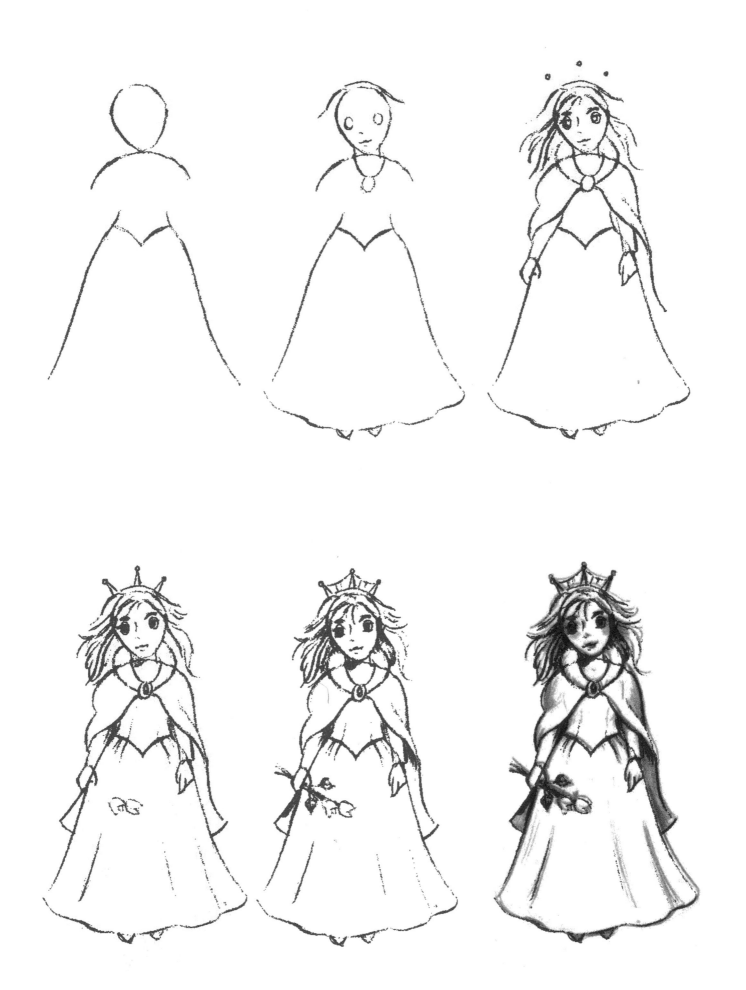

Teenage Princess

Eliza, the Handmaiden

Snow White

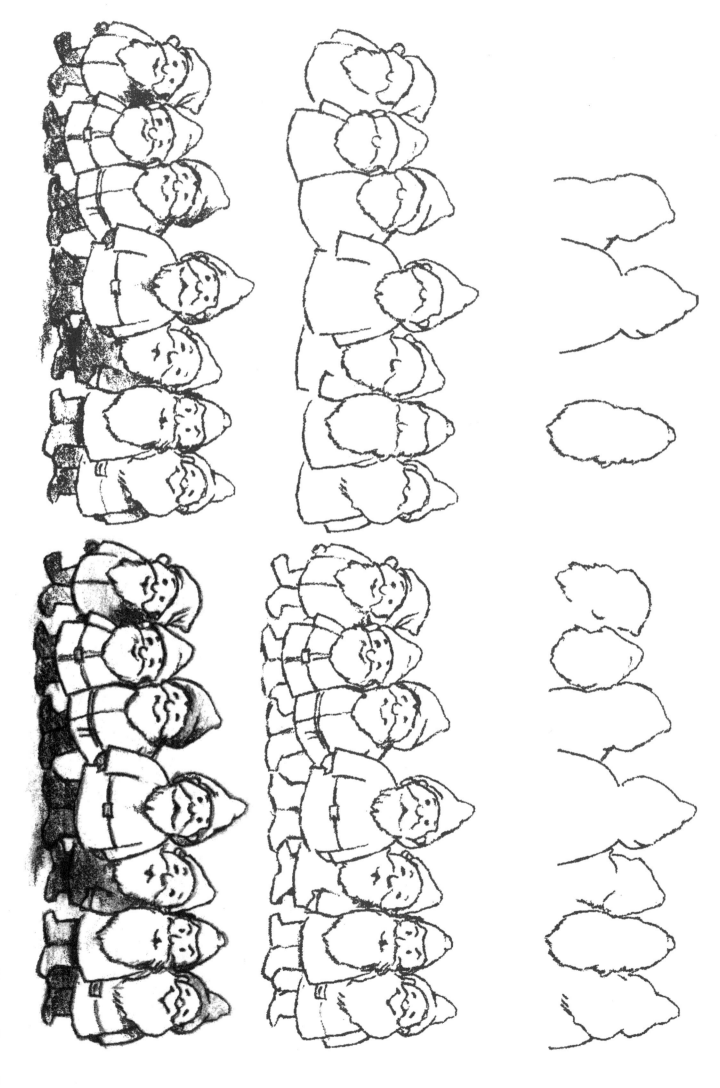

Seven Dwarfs

Poisoned Apple

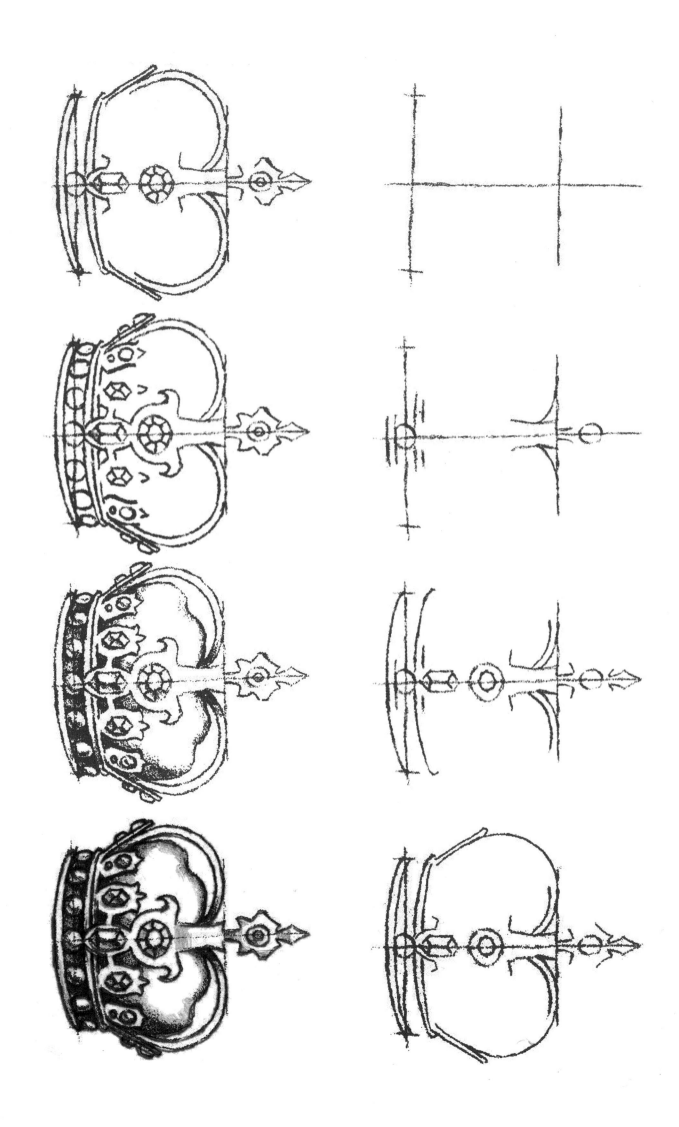

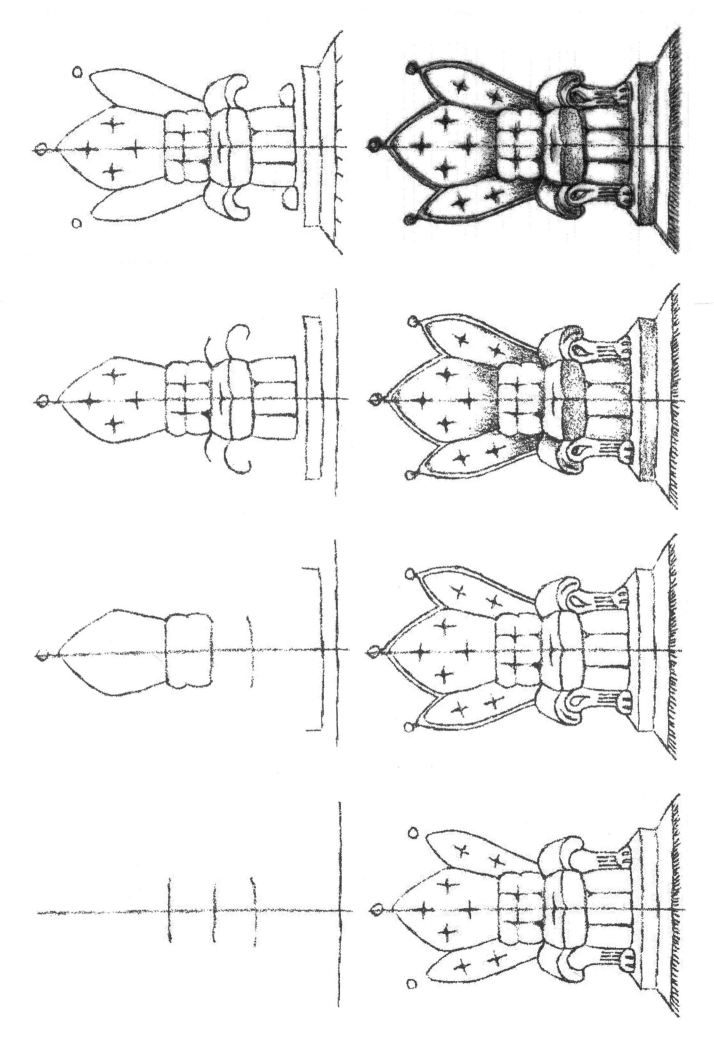

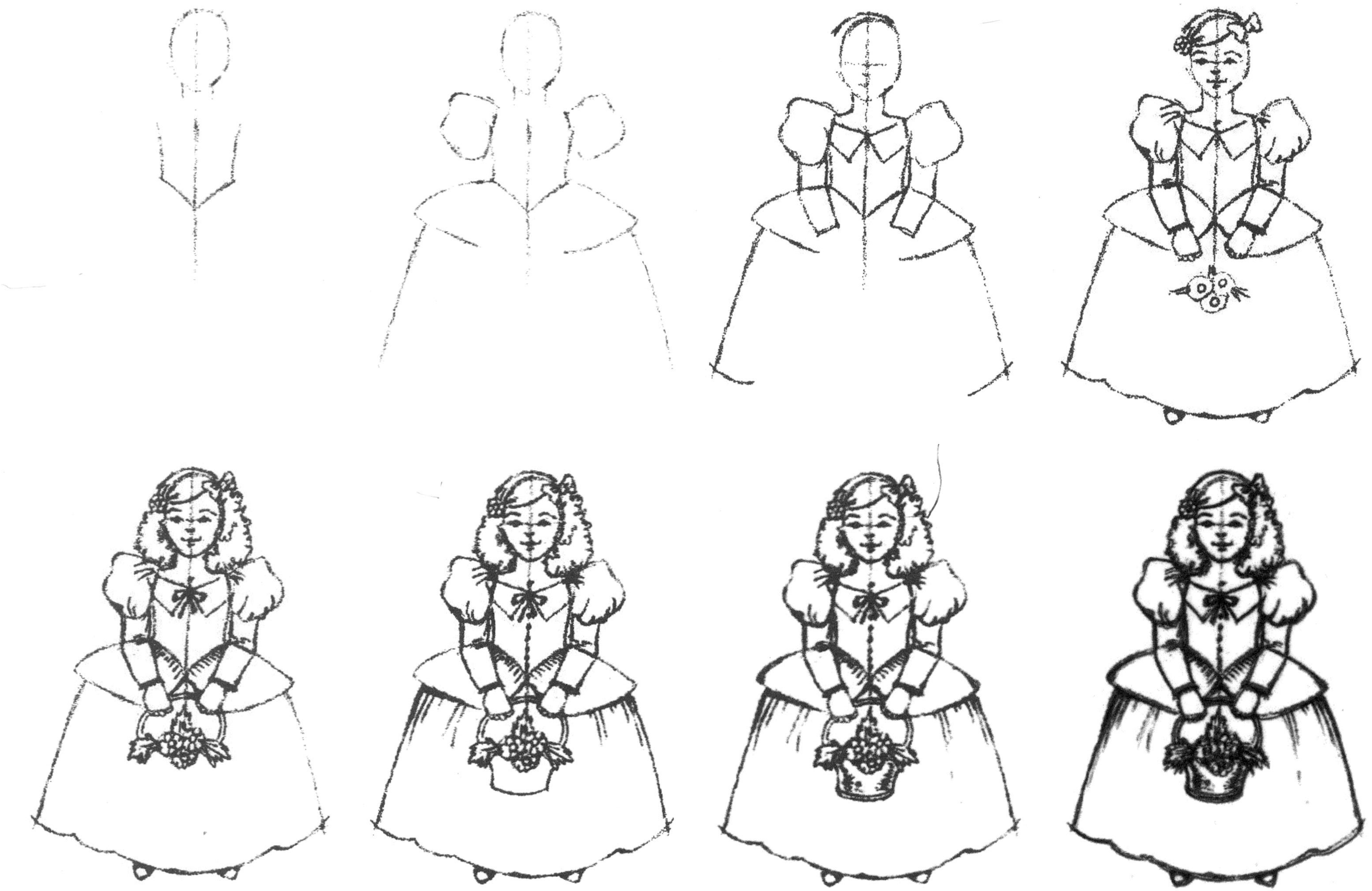

Young Princess

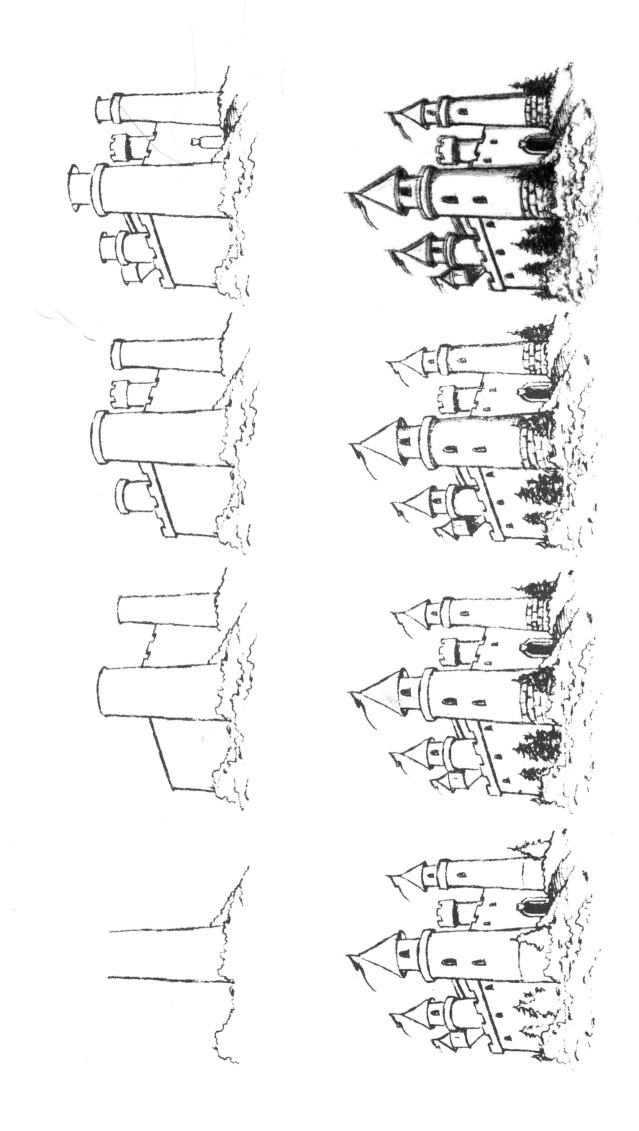

Japanese Princess

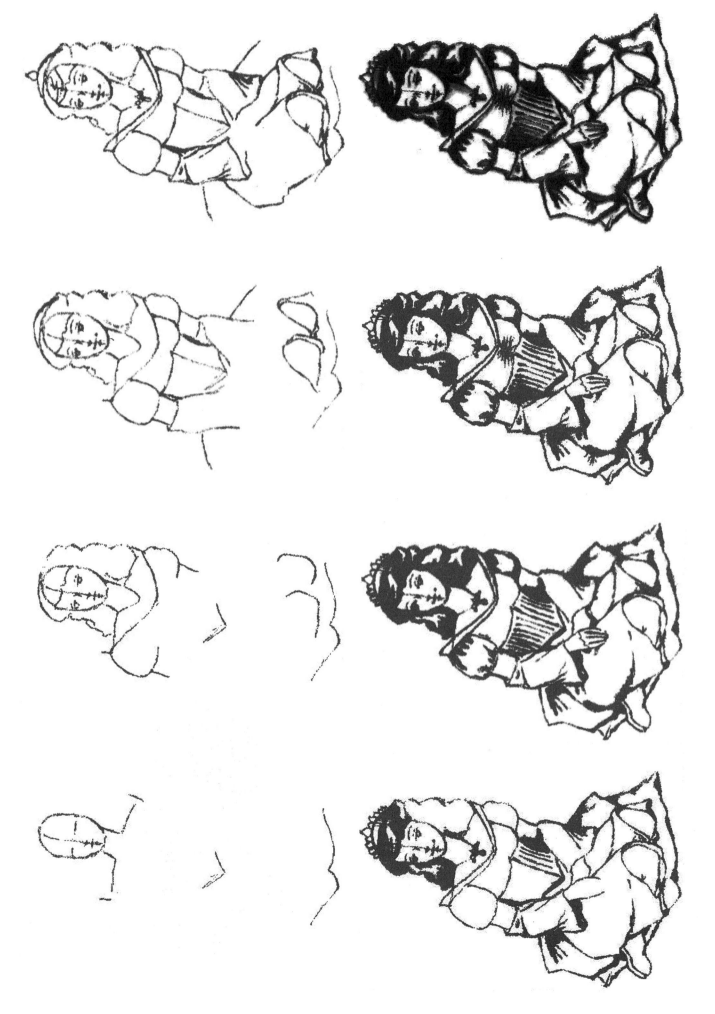

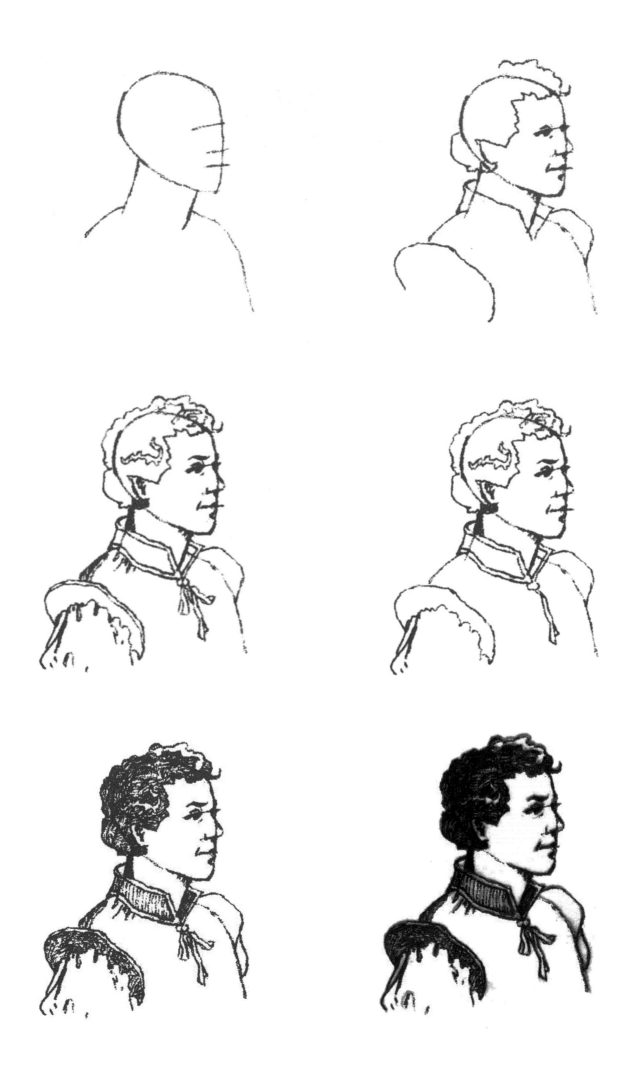

Romeo

Juliet

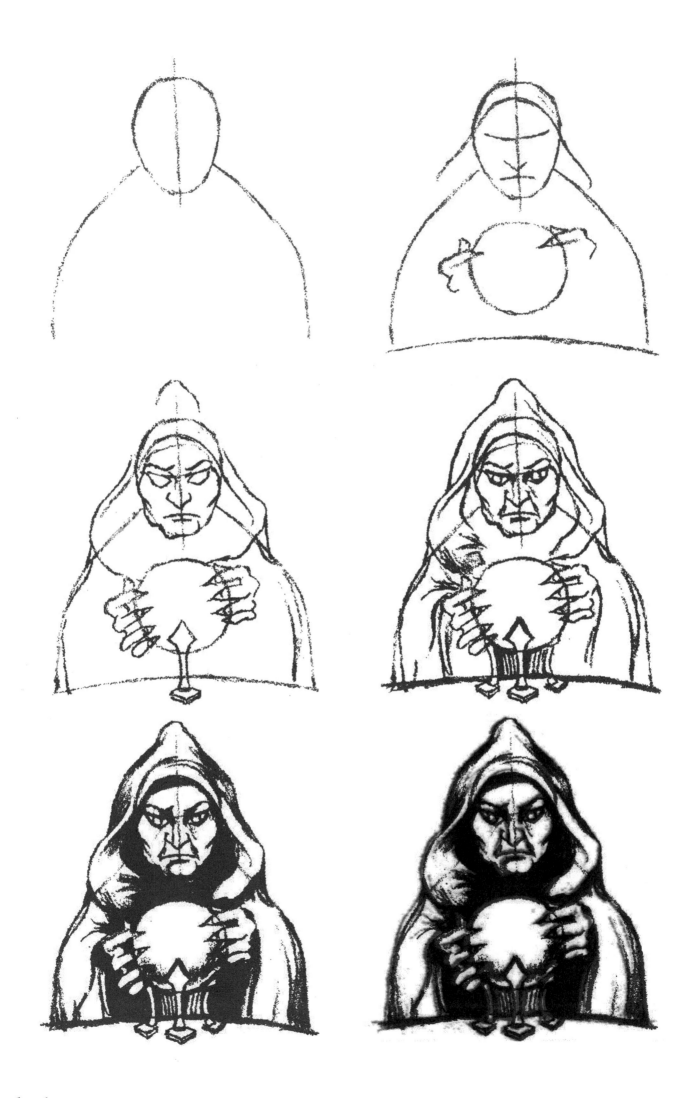

Warlock

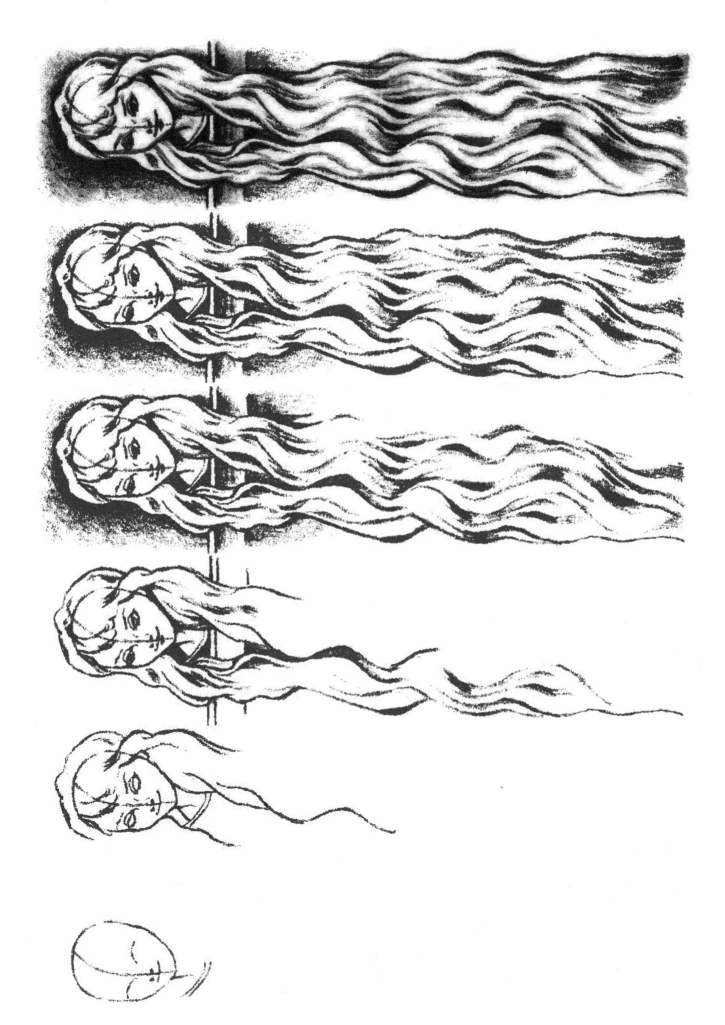

Princess Lilybet (Queen Elizabeth, Age 3)

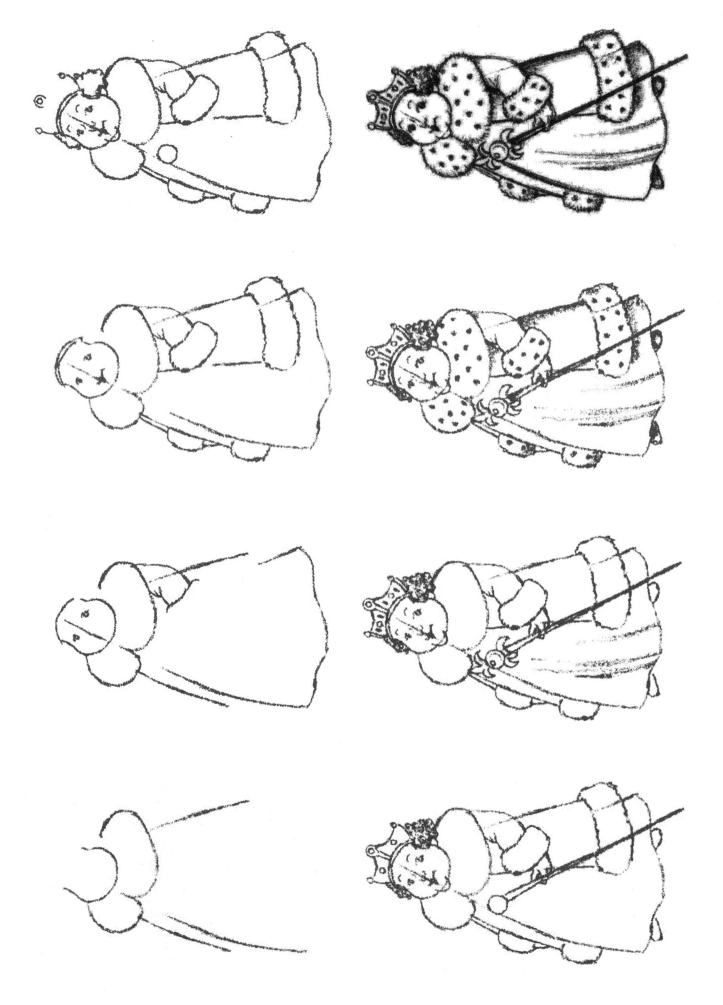

King Goodheart

Lightning (His Majesty's favorite mount)

Palace Jester

Dancing Princess

Squire

Frog Prince

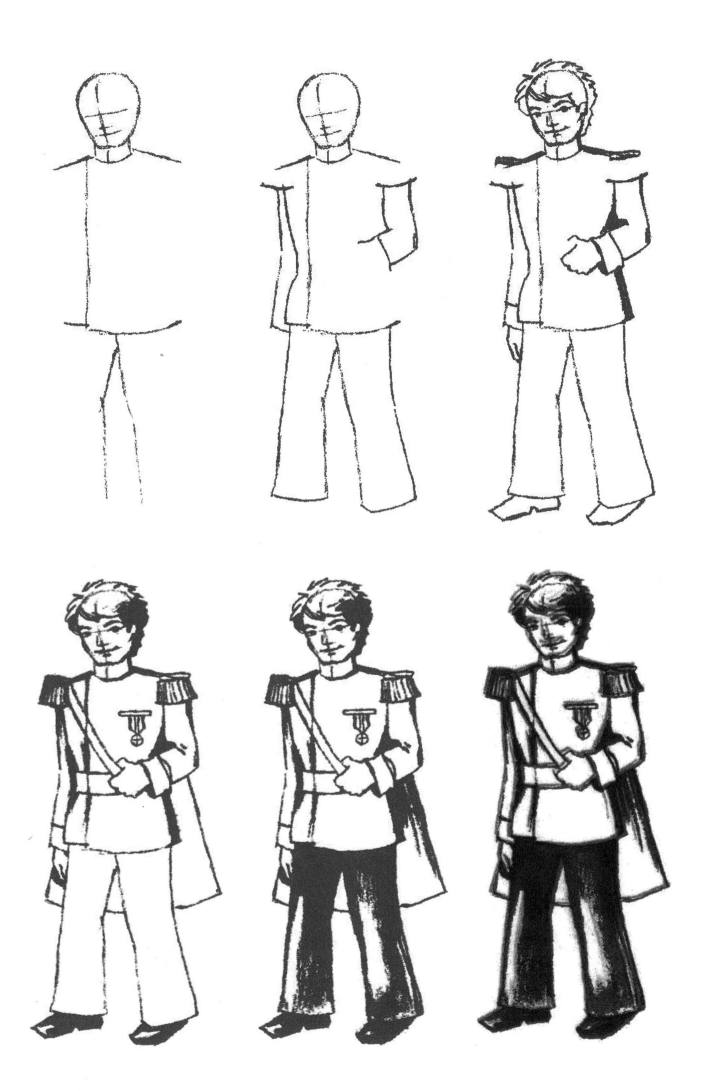

Prince

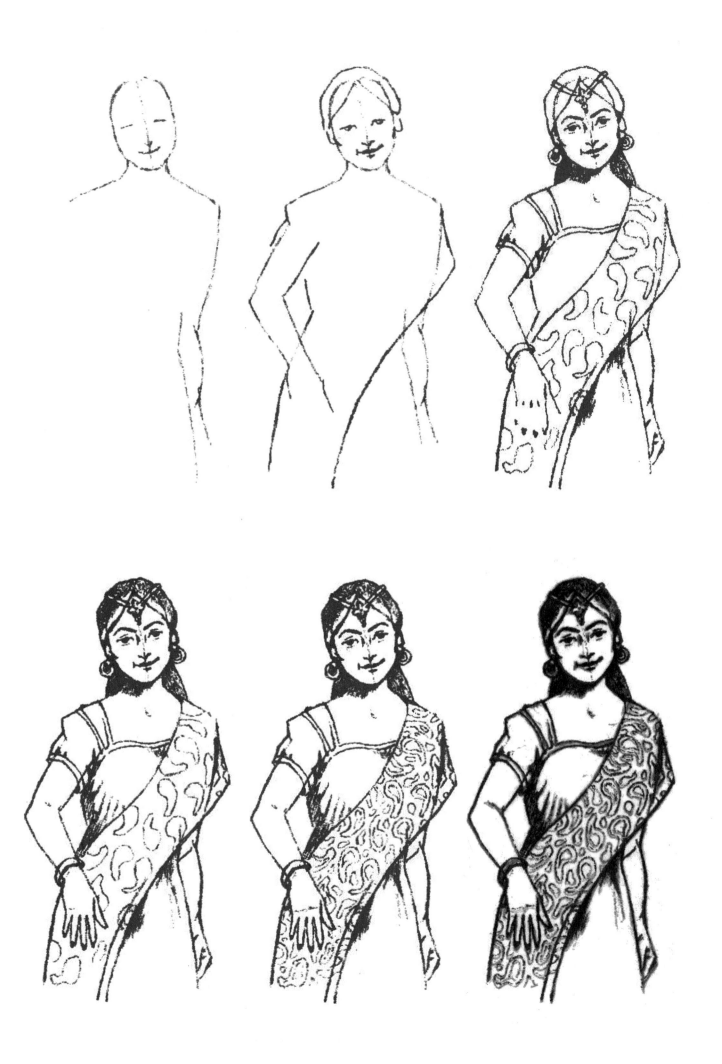

Indian Princess

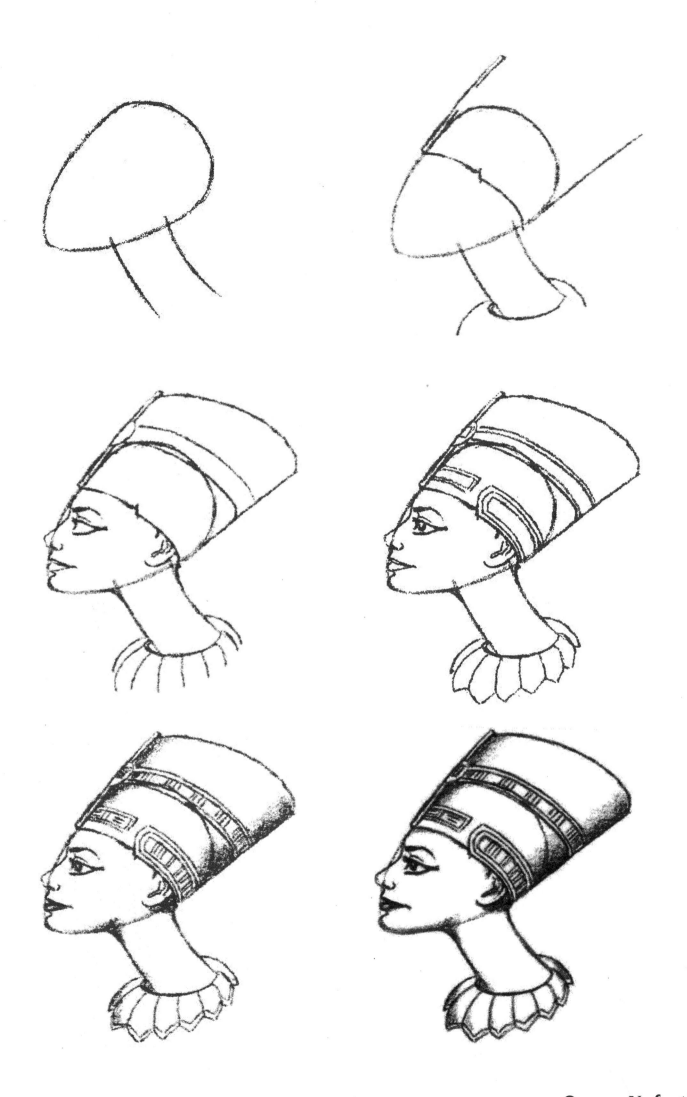

Queen Nefertiti

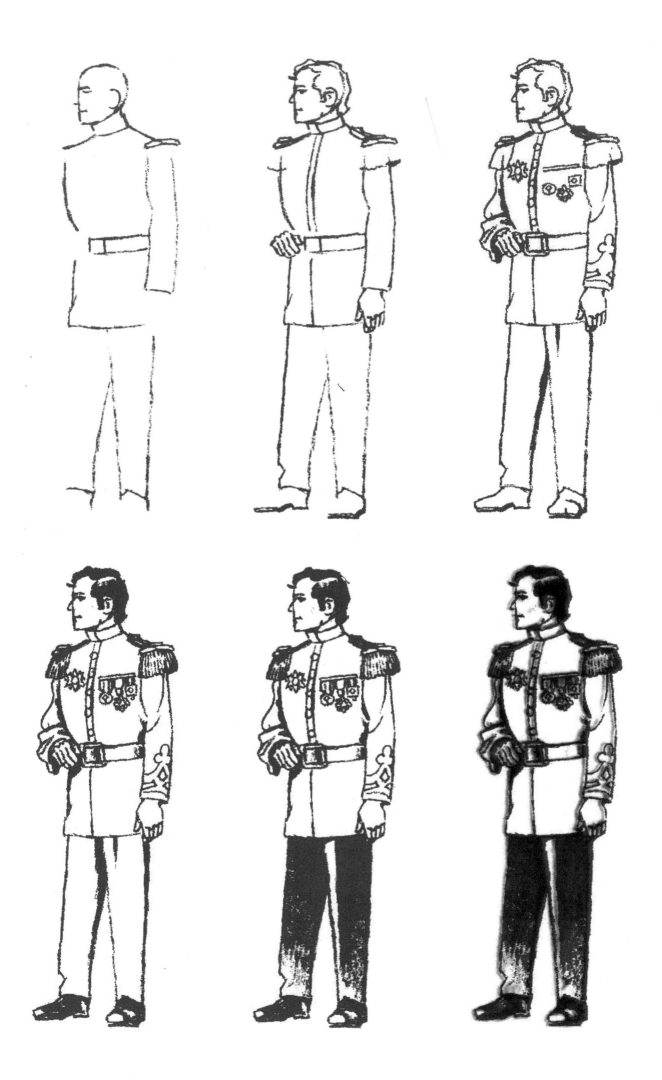

Prince Charming

Sleeping Beauty

African Princess

ABOUT LEE J. AMES

I've been married to Jocelyn for fifty-nine-plus years (either I'm lucky or I must have been doing something right). I have a son, Jonathan (his wife's name is Cynthia), and a daughter, Alison (her husband is Marty). I have three grandkids named Mark, Lauren, and Hilary. And I dare not omit our two magnificent hybrid canines, Missy and Rosie. All of the above are the makings of my lovely adventure!

Me? At eighteen I got my first job, at the Walt Disney Studios. Counting travel time across the country, that job lasted three months. I've been cashing in on the glory ever since! I've worked in animation, advertising, comic books, teaching, and illustrating books (about 150). I'm the author of more than thirty-five books (mostly the Draw 50 series). All have helped me happily avoid facing reality. We now live in the paradise of Southern California, but I still maintain membership in the Berndt Toast Gang, New York's chapter of the National Cartoonists Society.

DRAW 50 FOR HOURS OF FUN!

Using Lee J. Ames's proven, step-by-step method of drawing instruction, you can easily learn to draw animals, monsters, airplanes, cars, sharks, buildings, dinosaurs, famous cartoons, and so much more! Millions of people have learned to draw by using the award-winning "Draw 50" technique. Now you can, too!

COLLECT THE ENTIRE DRAW 50 SERIES!

The Draw 50 Series books are available at your local bookstore, or you may order them online at www.randomhouse.com.

ISBN	TITLE	PRICE
0-385-23629-8	Airplanes, Aircraft, and Spacecraft	$8.95/$13.95 Can
0-385-49145-X	Aliens	$8.95/$13.95 Can
0-385-19519-2	Animals	$8.95/$13.95 Can
0-7679-0544-X	Animal 'Toons	$8.95/$13.95 Can
0-385-24638-2	Athletes	$8.95/$13.95 Can
0-7679-1284-5	Baby Animals	$8.95/$13.95 Can
0-385-26767-3	Beasties and Yugglies and Turnover Uglies and Things That Go Bump in the Night	$8.95/$13.95 Can
0-385-47163-7	Birds	$8.95/$13.95 Can
0-385-23630-1	Boats, Ships, Trucks, and Trains	$8.95/$13.95 Can
0-385-41777-2	Buildings and Other Structures	$8.95/$13.95 Can
0-385-24639-0	Cars, Trucks, and Motorcycles	$8.95/$13.95 Can
0-385-24640-4	Cats	$8.95/$13.95 Can
0-385-42449-3	Creepy Crawlies	$8.95/$13.95 Can
0-385-19520-6	Dinosaurs and Other Prehistoric Animals	$8.95/$13.95 Can
0-385-23431-7	Dogs	$8.95/$13.95 Can
0-385-46985-3	Endangered Animals	$8.95/$13.95 Can
0-385-19521-4	Famous Cartoons	$8.95/$13.95 Can
0-385-23432-5	Famous Faces	$8.95/$13.95 Can
0-385-47150-5	Flowers, Trees, and Other Plants	$8.95/$13.95 Can
0-385-26770-3	Holiday Decorations	$8.95/$13.95 Can
0-385-17642-2	Horses	$8.95/$13.95 Can
0-385-17639-2	Monsters	$8.95/$13.95 Can
0-385-41194-4	People	$8.95/$13.95 Can
0-385-47162-9	People of the Bible	$8.95/$13.95 Can
0-385-26768-1	Sharks, Whales, and Other Sea Creatures	$8.95/$13.95 Can
0-7679-2076-7	The Draw 50 Way	$8.95/$13.95 Can
0-385-14154-8	Vehicles	$8.95/$13.95 Can

BROADWAY BOOKS